CW00631383

THE RESTRUCTURE

CHRIS MCCABE was born in Liverpool in 1977. His poetry collections are *The Hutton Inquiry* and *Zeppelins*. He has recorded a CD with The Poetry Archive and written a play *Shad Thames, Broken Wharf*, which was performed at the London Word Festival and subsequently published by Penned in the Margins in 2010. He works as a Librarian at The Poetry Library, London, and often tutors for The Poetry School.

Also by Chris McCabe

POETRY

The Hutton Inquiry
Zeppelins

PLAYS
Shad Thames, Broken Wharf

THE
RESTRUCTURE

by

CHRIS MCCABE

SALT

LONDON

PUBLISHED BY SALT PUBLISHING
Acre House, 11–15 William Road, London NW1 3ER, United Kingdom

All rights reserved

© Chris McCabe, 2012

The right of Chris McCabe to be identified as the
author of this work has been asserted by him in accordance
with Section 77 of the Copyright, Designs and Patents Act 1988.

This book is in copyright. Subject to statutory exception
and to provisions of relevant collective licensing agreements,
no reproduction of any part may take place without the written
permission of Salt Publishing.

Salt Publishing 2012

Printed in Great Britain by the MPG Books Group, Bodmin and King's Lynn

Typeset in Paperback 9 / 13

*This book is sold subject to the conditions that it shall not,
by way of trade or otherwise, be lent, re-sold, hired out,
or otherwise circulated without the publisher's prior consent
in any form of binding or cover other than that in which
it is published and without a similar condition including this
condition being imposed on the subsequent purchaser.*

ISBN 978 1 84471 426 1 hardback

1 3 5 7 9 8 6 4 2

LET ME SAY, since the day he was born
my son has brought me a black bird feather,
a blade of grass with human hair,
a smile in a petri-dish, a crutch of shit,
a heart that echoes with his lips.
When he speaks I captivate an audience.
Let me say, never before have I received this.

                        for Pavel

She uses the shreds of her dress for floss.
Let's see what tomorrow unearths.
It's her line that counts
like nightskies the canines close
not her void, to be filled
but a line of how she's conceived
– when she opens to speak   the stars of her

                        for Sarah

Contents

Acknowledgements

These poems, or versions of them, were published in the following magazines and ezines – thanks go to all of the editors :

Broadside [New Zealand]; *dwang*; *erbacce*; *Gists & Piths*; *LIT Journal* [US]; *Long Poem Magazine*; *The Manhattan Review* [US]; *NOON : Journal of the Short Poem* [Japan]; *Painted, Spoken*; *Poetry International Web*; *The Rialto*; *Salt Magazine*; *The Sampler*; *Shadowtrain*; *Spine*; *Succour*.

'Cornwall in 3 Trimesters' was commissioned by Isobel Dixon, Benjamin Morris and Helen Mort for a project on the Ceremonial Counties of the UK and was performed on St George's Day 2009.

'Nettles' was commissioned by James Wilkes for the *Herbarium* anthology (Capsule Press, 2011) and was read at Urban Physic Garden as part of that launch event on Friday 22nd July 2011.

Poems have also appeared in the following anthologies, *City State : New London Poetry* (Penned in the Margins, 2009); *Identity Parade : new British & Irish poets* (Bloodaxe 2010); *The Reiver's Stone* (Ettrick Forest Press 2010); *Soul Feathers : an anthology to support the work of Macmillan Cancer Support* (Indigo Dreams, 2011), *The Best British Poetry 2011* (Salt, 2011) and *The Robin Hood Book : poets in support of the Robin Hood Tax* (Caparison, 2012)

The whole of the THE RESTRUCTURE sequence has been recorded for The Poetry Archive.

Thanks go to Roddy Lumsden for editorial advice and proofreading.

I saw your name in italic bold
on the structure charts –

ringfence your thoughts
before you speak

you might find your face slip
on the pillow as you wake.

THE RESTRUCTURE is near
I think this is it

are you a delegator
or a chancer?

The structure is no longer
a vertical pipe

but a virtual funnel in which ideas
float to the top.

THE RESTRUCTURE is coming
like a central line tube

that plays industrial hardcore –
is there room in your ears

for subliminal messaging?
For echoes of past promises?

Are you a commuter
or a non-believer?

Time to play I Spy with the 'cc' field
are you in, are you out?

In the Silicon Valley of the blind
receiver, the politically aware are king.

Repeat : the politically naïve
are queen.

Are you a floater
or a sinker?

It's just this stress, lack of sleep –
thanks though, the chamomile helps.

THE RESTRUCTURE is coming
like a laminated airship of doom

if I could shift this headache, it reaps
and repeats, must be this monitor.

THE RESTRUCTURE is here
like rhinoceros euthanasia

even the thick skinned are tetchy –
did you see those armpit rings?

This is THE RESTRUCTURE
don't shoot the messenger –

have you seen the artistic porno?
You only get paid if you hold

your own. After all,
the organisation

is a cardio body
for staff, see Appendix

A First Wish

Waxleaf shadows
dapple the face
of our first unborn
upon the wall.

(Scans show, at just three months,
his face through aqueous radio).

Our shoes once cast pods in the snow
– we knew, only we knew –
I held you in bed like I'd only ever been shadow,
my palm made circles above your womb
like a lamp-wish in the dark to make a boy.

We never meant harm to anyone else
so new, we knew

rats outside mistaken for birds

our first dawn chorus
was all we knew to wish for

It was without reference
but I still drew axes of my emotions

I thought what I thought
would one day show me, but
there was no preposition, no question –
we had never been in love before.

We sought provisions to stay up all night –
my dad by chance losing his language
down aisles of red wine –
all night, to stay up, for electioneerings –
but the electric passed us into dark.

By candle-light the radio swirled us a station,
Mandelson said – a live statement, just for us –
I'm a fighter, not a quitter.

Our protean faces laughed in the patter-shadows

The landlady is knocking at the door & our bodies are locked
she's looking through the window & we're naked

(we never had landlords, that's a false hegemony).

When I read your copy of *Madame Bovary*
I'd never seen notes make such conversation
with a book before – a dialogue among equals –
left no doubt as to how Emma would have climbed
rungs of property ladders, accusations such as
what a bitch or *that's a bit sick really.*

Silenced asleep beside electric light

you sleep though the flutters beneath my palm

without   reference

this dawn chorus of lamp-moths

The meter ticked over   under cathedral floodlights
the amphetamines had worked & turned us to ice

I was on the pull-down flipseat (advert cancelled)
absorbing the lamp-lit galaxy we'd passed,

you said *I just want you to like me* I said : I do.
Then to be sure :   I do   I do   I do.

The driver paid us in vouchers printed : marriage
START : Barking   END : Barcelona

and I still didn't know what my name in your breath
would sound like in the dark –

I showed you photographs of me & some bachelors
(in the snow) & gave you something to sleep in

the come-down turned the ice to grit

(we meant no harm to anyone, my T-shirt your pillow)

The Rules Of Attraction

The rules of attraction are : it's
happening. The rules of attraction
are : red. The rules of attraction
are : time cuts a hand. The rules of
attraction are : common ground is
sliding. The rules of attraction are :
counterfeit. The rules of attraction
are : conception. The rules of att
raction are : amendments of your
self for someone who doesn't know
you. The rules of attraction are :
adrenalin pours sodium glutamate.
The rules of attraction are : honestly.
The rules of attraction are : reddish.
The rules of attraction are : miscon
ception. The rules of attraction are
: amend ————————————

The one rule of attraction is that it has already happened.
The one rule of attraction is deception.
The one rule of attraction is time cuts.
The one rule of attraction is already ash.
The one rule of attraction is rules.
The one rule of attraction is no rules.
The one rule of attraction is your pulse macarenas at the
    Reichstag.
The one rule of attraction is it will never happen.

You lifted your neck back to ask, the dog collar's metal
studs did a FIND&REPLACE on the stars. The interpreter

once reached out & touched me in the white stasis of the underground – I had no reason to hear after that. Wolfwhistled at plasticine for years. The tale began of a hackney cab & a Princess, the orange lights went back on & the white pills made tears in the cubicle. It was like we had jumped the queue on falling in. Leave. Stay for one more.

The rules of attraction are : it's already happened.

Housemates, Or How It Starts

Rapid Eye Movements riffled their deck

I must have just nod . . .

a Fritz Lang on the screen

– I think it was the screen –

it could have been a variant on my recurrent

dream of the vampyre in the oven

which had played on loop

in my sleep for 23 years,

then we were in the bachelor housemate's bedroom

(this was real)

trying to negotiate a sale on his double oak bed

still unmade in its box,

he imagined that by just putting it together

he could lie down with what we had found,

the room was dark except for a bottle of tequila

in the corner, a stripe of lizard green

with the worm playing dead just to spite us,

he tried to confuse the issue –

I'm not getting involved when he comes round here kicking off –

I said that won't happen, he's not like that.

He snorted cynical derision from both nostrils

so I knew this was really about him not having a woman.

I tried a different tact – *forget what I said –*

Look Anthony we're tired, we're two halves the same –

I know you've read Plato's Symposium –

so please just sell us the fuckin bed

This is THE RESTRUCTURE
we've been here before

like déjà vu is an annual dog biscuit
a clock that only ticks

when you wear shades.
THE RESTRUCTURE socialises

like a child reared in an elevator
up & down with bipolar adrenalin

as if the real world is only gravity
and other people – *I meant to ask*

how do the numbers relate
to the rumours?

All aboard for THE RESTRUCTURE
to sail is to oscillate

between credit & pocket crumbs,
a vessel that's ribbed

with xylophones & fish
that swims in the wrong key

like a stickleback harmonica,
a small organ of mouth gestures.

I saw your name on the charts
in underlined arial, think you're next,

at least that's what I saw, what she said,
don't shit on the messenger.

THE RESTRUCTURE is a manager
that multitasks myth & function

like a crucifix razor
with aloe vera

translates itself like the wrongly
acquitted, seethes breathily

as the workplace nutcase.
You have to accept the fact

that THE RESTRUCTURE is as unbelievable
as a fictional giro, presents

the crunch as just a visa-dunky
that swirls a paisley residue

for each curled sip, says Yes
when it means No

like a Liberal's sphincter, wipes
its pretty black boots on the chessboard

to put the white squares asleep,
makes plastic pawns of once

porous kings, asks for advice
whilst instructing the action –

I meant to say I saw some words
xeroxed downwards :

THE RESTRUCTURE wants you to individuate
by doing exactly what it says

Break Of Day

It's only lights out when you close your eyes,
their amber of yes; eyes
in nakedness still the most part of you,
that you could walk into this room
as dominatrix or lost French maid
and wet, looking behind,
the game would be over –
as the nights draw in the biggest climax ever
you fall asleep in pink across my knees,
I cover you against the cold with no gain to myself,
to my own eyes; the clock like a Barratt crane
builds towards a city decimated, decrowned,
we are forced to leave as another night closes
down. *Perfect sexual love* was the phrase we found to use,
living too late this does us justice
the crows' feet ingrained across my face
as evidence that this took place,
I cannot sleep longer than two hours
without speaking across & hearing us,
scents left on your body even as it tires
residues of imagination, desires,
when morning makes this lost & the gales
rotate the dreams we've shared to genesis,
across gardens blankets collapse
as interiors after sleep-walked violence,
strange what the sun each day brings to us –
I never believe night past until we enter this.

The Pure knows that these are the bliss days.
You say you want this weekend to last forever,
Sundays are endless houses with boards FOR SALE,
your purple poncho drifts the industrial estate
(a crocus we saw in the cracks of the Reichstag),
shredded names form our breath & remain –
Echo, Daphne, Iris / Pavel, Kester, Blaise.
Spring gives the nights less to get lost in,
already on the doorstep a sun of foxing amber
sucks its dogfox offspring into its rays,
a gimpshow of shredded binbags across the street –
a pure pearl bulb & eight dud teabags.

When I thought I'd lost the notebook of these poems
it was like the months had never taken place,
nights of imagined tics scratched off the back
of the year, like Herrick's vision –
Night to the Record! that was all,
but there it was left under the scanner
open to hear of the pregnancy Yes –
litmus tongue pronged pink in a perfect plus.
When we tested twice does that make twins?
From perfect sexual love our babes are buds,
but The Pure wants you still in silky pinks –
Love give me more such nights as these.

THE RESTRUCTURE witchdoctors
obsolete policies into greetings cards

records cases of volatile sickness
on C60 cassettes

breathes its shortbread lurgy
to make sure the punters are awake

and when it's here, THE RESTRUCTURE
outsources the nightwatch

freelancing mosquitoes to vampyres,
wires alarms to spitoons

for the saline dawnchorus
and when the backlash shimmers

does away with cages to dunk
fresh swallows in ramekins of mud

offers 5 free mystery tattoos
that reveal to read

BRING ON THE RESTRUCTURE
or I'M IN YOU WILL BE TOO

puts children's teeth on edge
by setting chrome in cotton candy

– can I suggest a contingency plan, if you're
still feeling like this tomorrow you're going nowhere –

you'll be watched by THE RESTRUCTURE
a squirrel disguised in a cloud of starlings

I don't know, what does it matter
– she thought the world of him –

as the crowd will disperse
in mud & claws & hostility

it's important that you listen for once :
THE RESTRUCTURE wants to think its world in you

Cornwall In 3 Trimesters

NO ELECTRIC BLANKETS / NO SHIRAZ / NO CATS / NO
X-RAYS / NO MICROWAVES / NO FISH / NO SMOKE / NO
MERLOT / NO CANNABIS / NO HOTDOGS / NO CAFFEINE /
NO REPTILES / NO WATER BEDS / NO PINOT GRIGIO / NO
PESTICIDES / NO PAINTS / NO CREAM TEAS / NO SUNRAYS

2

After the broken *hymen* in *honeymoon*,
the rogue *id* in *stupid*
and how we had slept like a dream
through a sleep with no dreams,
and Barcelona had prepped him
Berlin sewn him (your cycle & lexicon
would not accept this) the boy-foetus
took the onus on himself
– no *prep*, didn't *sew* – used instead
his spine to saw your ribs
and after we'd replaced *tannins* with *units*
to briefly taste the erasure of the second bottle,
was it taboo to confess that pregnancy
was a trope we dreamt into obsolescence
like the invisible cloak of the Renaissance stage –
a stasis endured for this collop of happiness?
One drink and I'm, like, yeh, the world is
your oyster but only if your fingers *shook*.
The boy-foetus was oneiric (under your ribs)
like a warted thumb in the mouth of a Geisha.
I walked up the escarpment to the B & B

(past the azaleas peppered with Nora's ashes)
for paracetamol, picked a wild poppy
through collapsed wire rails, the room
as we had left it – Nabokov's short stories,
the sun cream – blanking the Atlantic with a shush.
Any of those cottages could be the family home
that Nora walked in to ask for 'two cream teas'.
Past the azaleas & shelves of *Greetings From*
and clotted creams – at the sealife centre –
flatfish stared sideways from the glass.
Pavel when you played boy-foetus
– hunched Hamlet in wait of a sea-change –
what did you dream in the amniotic fizz?

Kidney scan eight dilated a whole drowned
map of Kernow, and if there's a special providence
in the fall of a sparrow, the sparrow (on screen)
was asleep in an honesty box, under closed-circuit
    surveillance.

3

NO SAUNA / NO HOT TUB / NO HOT BATH / NO CAT LITTER
/ NO UNCOOKED MEATS / NO CAMEMBERT / NO HERPES /
NO PEANUT BUTTER / NO HARD SEX / NO TIGHT JEANS / NO
UNDERWIRE BRAS / NO VACCINATIONS / NO HAIR DYES /
NO FLYING / NO AROMATHERAPY / NO CONTACT SPORTS /
NO BELGIAN LAGERS / NO LATE NIGHTS / NO STRESS

30th Birthday, Musselburgh

And sat under the papier-mache mermaid,
the table an afterlife of seafood –
like your first memory : starfish
along the railway tracks.
Purple flints in the emptied wineglass –
for so long pregnant, frosted finger-tacks.
Our baby's head grinds itself under your ribs –
above the table, an atlas on its latches.
Then you're pale in the wings of the dressing-table
mirror, a Victorian on amphetamines.
And this is how we find ourselves somewhere –
the harbourside town of Musselburgh
outside the boarding school for 18 year olds
it makes me glad to be working class
I'd rather have no money & be free.
That oyster, this plate, will bit-part a new life –
but what will the world make of the cells under
a mother's ribs, already having formed themselves?

Midnought

Still unsure if I believe in luck, or ghosts,
I have been unlucky as 13 erotic ghosts.

I started smoking the day before the ban & loved
the cigarette stumps like crushed drummer-boys.

This & other kinds of bitterness pitted a kitsch beauty –
I carried a retro sports bag full of lemons & roses.

Digital zeros at midnight like amphetamine owls –
she says : *You can never escape the Taxi Man*

(outside two feet crucified by flip-flop
echo & knock against the night black).

At midnight, online, she checks a balance transfer,
I read a book from a dead man's collection –

her magazine shows the outline of a model in the far flush
of pregnancy, a snail that climbs a salted branch.

Week 31 Scan

Already the clip-curls of your hair roll ringlets of smoke,
fingers dance week-long memories of self-discovery
dactyls that glyph new letters –

the bête-noire of your being – right kidney
in reflux – lazy bat that sleeps all night.

Scan tunes in to the back you turn clockwise
to confuse the doctor, he says, *this child confounds me.*

Will you always turn your back like this, to confound?

Mouth of a top-feeder takes practice breaths,
sucks amniotic gulps in readiness for air –

when each breath's reverb latches an echo in speech

in reflex

you will know how hard it's been to say this

And so, THE RESTRUCTURE says :
this is the finger food with rohypnol dip

and next to that the urban carcass
with citrus & amphetamines

– a wren that blings –
– a swift that headspins –

I don't want to risk the commute
I feel much better but it could finish me off.

Each child is fitted with earplugs
to make phonetic tasks more of a challenge

and when THE RESTRUCTURE changes eyes
with sugarcubes to watch the stars dissolve

writes out affidavits – I THE RESTRUCTURE –
spank the mackerel to copyright omega-3

speed-eat with sailors moored against land
use OCD to paperclip oysters

lay wasp pupa inside caterpillars
and eat sibling foeti with a shark's

internal promotion smirk – allow exoskeletons
to be frozen in the ecosystem on application –

it's a good offer, thank you Mr Banker
but I'm going to risk one more round –

then employ a CGI expert to rewind
all loft clocks to hang on walls

like a home is a bandit windfall
that oscillates bilaterally in the mind –

I once went to a kebab shop with a pub
in the back, the people were happy but they had no money

it reminds THE RESTRUCTURE of its humble starts
barrowboying the fruit & veg ATM

shouting *any old iron* when it meant *papermoney*
when it socialised to ensure the whole pub ended

at the supplies' store for newly printed priests,
innovated the hours of retina clicks

to find the function to fit the purpose
– a handheld in a teapot –

but is now kind enough to offer emotional feedback
in primary colours for those who don't like *the truth*

and as stress depletes & colleagues enjoy air-con compliments
THE RESTRUCTURE offers the bereft their own chance of success

The Midwitches

are sorcerers between science & prophecy,
prick at bone heels to lumin four red moons.
Go door-to-door as sales-people of health
and five portions of frightful vag.
Hands mole over wombs, a search for
armadillos with the shells removed.
Eavesdroppers of heartbeats, a swoosh
of black boots on a poppy tarmac.
So much care taken over sutures to sew
women back together, as if labia
is the label in the pubic sweater.
100% flesh. Keep away from fire.
Grey fusili cord uncoiled & cut with clippers
red-metallic, to be auctioned as keyrings.
Trolley dollies of pethidine & pleaded-for
pain in the hold-up at placenta patisserie.
Then you left the room : came back
to a hijacked child suckling on pork
popsicles of piglets. A midwife called Star
with such advice as : eat pineapple
to make the contractions start. A trade
secret on how to start the woman off –
a hook on a long silver stick. You thought
that was medieval until they unveiled
the weights of sugar-balanced silver scales.
Pessaries inserted with a card dealer's
confidence, smoke potions up the flesh flue
they chant & turn to face you –
a postnatal door opens a room – a cage of film-noir –
a creel of white hair strung up in the rails.

The Birth

Head stuck, Chilean miner,
wet fontanelle butting on air,
midwives whispering conspiracies
– we were so happy why did we do this –
inhaled gas, sd : to be fair – this is good shit :
handed me the mask for a hit : I'm okay, I'll pass :
my one task forever now to keep synapses clear, for you,
and for his – who I'd still never seen – defence. I'll stick to oxygen.

Compressed root pushed outwards
in a mush of flesh & placenta
flexed to miracle : pushed deltoids
up to look into your face – the one
who had whispered to him in the jolting dark.
Late for work, listening to Rammstein
across Blackfriars Bridge – clock card
of morse – landed on the soft pillar
of your stomach, the skin to his mind,
and locked your eyes like your eyes
were a mirror reading his mind. His
muscles limber as seaflowers so how
did he wide-arm press-up to raise
himself to see you, his face bruised
and swollen as a festive squash,
papier-mache boxer, eyes seal-wet,
clip curls of hair in branches of seahorses.

In the ward, three of us – new maths –
I unparcelled his feet like the king's pastries
and asked if you would like to reconsider what filos

our bones. The instant test of his ears – sparrow's
larynx, a modified toy orchestra – all clear in seconds.

> The ward like a vending machine
> accepting blood pulse for cash –
> the boy hears!
> Give us the silence of that first success.

THE RESTRUCTURE drowns cats in paperbags
feeds catnip to domestic mice

oscillates between reopening & closure
to prove the truth of Freud's fort-da game

makes offers in exchange for silence,
asks : will there be a leaving do

before the redundancy deal?
THE RESTRUCTURE is louche in style

non-piffling in size, repetitive in nature,
in nature a reptile of louche style

approaches domestic situations
from 5 perspectives, even in square rooms

mistakes gluesticks for cigars –
Now listen, thanks for helping with this

we could get fucked & though you won't get a cut
the individual stands to get a one percent split.

Over-then-over for THE RESTRUCTURE
committing with hard copy proposals

backs itself into a corner like a homemade thriller,
postulates its shadow tremulously

like a funeral latecomer bearing gifts
of red pansies in a kidney dish

plays host to the candles for your final wish
then blows the leaf flames in your face

with an anaesthetist's swazzle,
writes a press release to announce any team-member's

stay in rehab, forwarding the landline to its mobile
to be first to know when they rehit the bottle

then makes you answer in a borrowed accent
– It's not like, that I dislike you or anything

we've just never clicked – then I saw THE RESTRUCTURE
shadow the outbreak of moths with a clump of red bricks

Paternity Leave

Railings outside hospitals, railings outside schools,
on a day commonplace as rain
a boy of three days sees light for the first time
– leaves of green, leaves of red, blow through steel –
as so many times the boy will say *I'm going home*

The basket weaves sunlight
pink fists punch the air
Hosannah! Hosannah!
The boy is brown-blonde
almost gold
like jaundice is an alchemy
for the chosen.
Down on the street, from the window,
an apple core in the gutter.
The basket contains birds
– one red, one green –
what's chosen in gold is *this* one
watching the sun come up
weaving the walls with rosettes of light

Then to learn the language of the pet shop
a choice of pedigree pups
– Jack Russells, shepherds, collies –
and written on cardboard, *ginger kittens*;

it's not the expense that counts :
if the boy prefers cats, it's easy to choose

Pavel : the name continues to give.

Diminutives generous.

Pashenka : baby.

Pasha : boy.

(Affectionate : Pavelchops, Pavelboots *etc*).

Russian-Slavic for Paul.

Little one.

Little Paul.

Sun smears a stained glass pink rose on the floor.

A baby is held in the window. Across the street

another baby is held in the window. Sun

smears stained glass blue swallows on the floor.

foxes cackle in the yard like starvation is a joke

lamb-bleats of a baby in his basket

(there is no choice when chosen to protect)

D IS FOR DINOSAUR

At ten p.m., on his fifth day, a syringe of antibiotics

– precautionary, for the black owl of the kidney –

The Blue Planet, somewhere out there, in digital, soothes –
    amniotic, hypnotic –

as if Attenborough is our paymaster –

the hatchlings, however, have already started out on their journey

[34]

Violent storms (the radio dictates)
off the shores of the British Isles,
squally showers at Berwick-upon-Tweed,
the gale outside groans against grains,
shunts down alleys –
how does the terrace sail (it is sailing)
moored as it is to market dynamics?

i'm on another planet

in   outer | SPACE |

three bottles make a triumvirate class approach :
tomato sauce . warm milk . champagne .

Out of the amniotic sac for twelve days
and held in the light & jingle of the penny arcade
a boy forgets to cry for his feed, caught in what
is red & green, hypnotic, synaesthetic –
in the digital portrait booth he stares back at himself
as the sketch of a photograph draws his face –

[35]

as if for the slot of creation
he wants to show how a coin gets made.

a spilt pool of baby milk
rippled with plum shiraz
a fine rich dessert for beginners,
so we start from that & end with *this*
and all we do is clasp our lips

Lamb-bleats of sleep

dragonsnorts of wind

a folklore we've made

of monsters & innocence,

the midwife told us

"You've brought a beautiful

baby into a crazy world"

but after birth, no one told us,

you only talk in mono-words.

Beautiful, we said. Crazy.

(On November the first

the world was waiting

in a car park *out there*)

There is a story of two little birds
– not a red bird & green bird –
but blackbirds called *kidneys*
and a lop-eared owl called *bladder*,
that made a bleep (tweet tweet)
at the anti-creche of machines,
made faces like trees at night
in black Os of puddles & eyes.
The story ends in amnesias of warm milk
as in silence, at last, the boy meets sleep.

where there is wind will be words

Red

Ten words for how she is : she said sorry for my pain as she gave
    birth.

On starry nights in December the jukebox was tendentious.
With the afterbirth arrived the text : *no more drinking for you* –
four weeks later the pram rolled on its own down the tube,
she took the can the drunk commuters offered her, alighted,
pointed towards Canary Wharf – which she hated – & said
                            "I fucking love this City".

She got off on Red the way I had on amphetamines,
I got off on The Word the way she did on Red.
Words for her brother : take the Northbound northwards & don't fail.

Red for her was what some hear in a name (names came in colours),
Red communist stars on the tree, so Christ was at rest.
She said Castro's brother was hardly Young Flesh, at the time
she was wearing a red T-shirt : UNWRAP ME FOR CHRISTMAS.
Talked of other red things : migrating to Wandsworth on the Central
               Line, a career as a socialist.
On Pay Days we went to the dogs & put it all on Trap 1
(the boy adrift in the boat of honey sailed away on a sea of sleep).
Trap 1 won. And Yes, she did look a little like the woman
          in Picasso's *Pierreuse, la main sur l'epaule*.

She accepted the can. The pram rolled down the tube.
She stood up in dark music & danced in red silks.
She carefully fed the child & poured more shiraz.
A vulva of red lipstick around the neck of the glass

a baby bottlenecked in a celluloid pool
emerged a clay doll – he breathes! –
& stunned us to the wall. His birthmark
– new borders – embossed in red on his neck.

THE RESTRUCTURE employs luminescent workmen
to rewire the leisure cables

to divert live bones into the A-road
to prepare the basket for the dogging session

with a bassett hound strapped
in the passenger seat –

I've heard Barbara's leaving, Janice
will probably get her job, then THE RESTRUCTURE

will sort out what's left for us, but did you see
the double lobes of debris explode

over the paperclips, and then to flatter
I heard THE RESTRUCTURE *cream up*

the PA saying her tight body
could have been made from starstuff

before throwing-up in its Sunday best
of hunt red & black bowler

tequila-starters hurled in pools
sloshed around galoshes

before wiping itself down to strut
its stuff in fresh gladrags

I couldn't believe what I saw.
THE RESTRUCTURE like a locum doctor

prescribing passwords *furry mushroom* & *canary pancake*
substantiating all available fields

such as *Look For* : Recognition, which trawls
the inbox archive like the system's software has the bends

and could be mistaken for a screw
except all its keys are bent out-of-usage

– Are we still allowed a teabreak
I always had one before, it's the time I take my pills –

THE RESTRUCTURE talks of *re*possessing your attention
as if to make clear that it owned your thoughts before

counts each multiple sneeze in its sleep
to replace wet dreams

wakes with the agenda prepared
for any disconnect in communication

– We do sort of sympathise with the stress
and you know, kind of want to help –

but whatever today's agreement with THE RESTRUCTURE is,
is tomorrow's obsolete eject

[41]

The Renaming

Freddy Hutchinson, Hutchado, Fredmondo, Choccytoes, Choxteth, General Wriggles, Crazy Gypsy, Powerhouse, Pavelhood, Schmiggleroyd, Tiggeroo, Koala Boy, Pavelchops, Pavelboots, Baby Strange, Little Big Boy, LBB, Mr Mister, Mister Boy, Baby Ness, Babski, Tall Paul, Tavel Pavel, Gadfly, Iris, Baby Fossil, Fossil-Schmiggs, Paulo-Lavrenti, PLC, Our Little Prince, Sonfriend, Cutoid, Bib Priest, Naan Bread, Baby Pure, Pavelsaurus, Lentilsuede, Dr Scrunchies, Viking, Makoshark.

Mr Schmiggles

Walked four miles to give 3,000 to the estate agents.
After the wait at the east end checkout we eat
jam sandwiches in the bluebottle static of the cemetery.
The child was named Mr Schmiggles, his forefinger
confounded science as we crossed from the hospital
into a public house called THE PERSEVERANCE
(he slept soundlessly through three bottles of red).

The communist child, we found, that receives
a piggybank at birth, hurls cubes of curdled milk
onto a Happy Pig bib. The finger was raised
through *Rapunzel* which seized the actor
to point back at Schmiggs – but speak instead
to the papier-mache shawl – *Get that baby out of here!*
He struggled to purse the red buds of his lips.

The doctor introduced Sir Roses of mud-brown liver
and mistaking Schmiggles for a Freddy Hutchinson
said : *We want to remove his head.* Schmiggles
closed the loveheart wishbone of his jaws
and with the thrash of a mako shark
clamped his mouth around the pitted soother
of his nose as he screeched *My God my proboscis!*

Then goes Schmiggs in polka dot mitts
orchestrating a mash-up between a giant bee
and the lyrics of Mark E. Smith.
In the electric chair of hiccoughs
like a Jack-in-the-Box with Tourettes,
a Rubik's cube of wind making itself red

in his stomach as he depuzzles flatulence.

Then Lord Schmiggles of Schmiggville retesting
the Schmiggleometer to avert a Schmiggle-ectomy
– schmig schmig schmig schmig – all schmigged-out
in the schmiggle machine waiting with a gurn in his eyes
for someone to start the journey : *Let us go then, you and I* . . .
Falls asleep with the latch off his dreams
black feet shuffling at the edge of consciousness.

On Christmas morning Schmiggs robed as Santa
and making a note of our hopes he sat on *our* knee.
Entered as Baron Von Schmiggles in Lindbergh collar
hitting the butter at the buffet bar, absorbed in his
first coloured lights like an ABC of amphetamines –
Christmas bulbs, full moon, blue swallows –
entranced with the digital Mozart of the green caterpillar.

We all want Cinderella to fall for Buttons but the lesson
is that the woman wants to dabble with The Prince.
We watched the drunks crab & morph in the fog
compelled homewards by anecdote & memory.
Sometimes Schmiggles was unsure how these things worked –
the toddler with an iron whip, the snowman saddled
on a Harley – wanting to know life – & melting to wet on the seat.

THE RESTRUCTURE leaves the strangest sensation
– a statue that's seen you naked –

lurks in the corner
like a really *rude* mugger

shimmers all water to filth
adumbrates the dark web

asks 'How am I looking?' four times
removing the question marks

like coathangers in lifejackets,
steams langoustines still wearing their shades

but rips outs the intestines like emergency
pullchords, arranges rock opera lightshows

for family & friends to get lost in
and lists bereavement meetings as *catchups*.

Whistles urban foxes at minus two degrees
then throws sponges at urinals to soak E. coli.

THE RESTRUCTURE plays host at motivational dinner-parties
using paper spatulas to not offend the chicken

creates a new borough called *urbia* between
all that's known by town planners & taxi drivers

employs bouncers to pay wages in olives
for those who turn up during speeches

creates its own school agenda
called THE RESTRUCTURE Silly Bus

which claims never to stop, even for
pertinent questioners, takes consistent users of irony

at their word to enforce the Disciplinary Policy
for phrase-searching "good clean fun" online.

THE RESTRUCTURE watches others get drunk
offering sample refills in mercury phials

but stops short when its own levels
start to slip on velvet

– You've got to start listening, this is getting serious
and most of what I'm saying I won't repeat –

THE RESTRUCTURE has offered you a baptism
in its subsidized black rivers

An ABC Of First Light

A MR TOAD PAELLA

For the monster paella she broke the ABC snail
into plastic chunks & shredded the green Velcro
of the caterpillar that sang Bach. She added every
thing – squirrel, meat, fish – as her temples pulsed
she ordered in the cast of *The Wind in the Willows*
– only Toad was out of contract & in he went –
(with the saffron & white wine fusing the taste
of decibels & lexicon). But the boy went looking
for his toys so we put him in the boat of honey –
the GREEK GODS wallchart had replaced
the quilt, the action too graphic for an undersheet
to fit. To pacify we tried a game of Communist
Monopoly, giving 200 euros to the one most in need
as they passed GO, organized small red houses
on a terraced basis. Some made it into the dish
which we knew was done when silence cancelled
Toad's new-corporate *Poops!*

BUTTERCUP

I put a buttercup under my chin & yellow vans go past –
some say RENEW GLASS, others SASH WINDOWS.
USB cables & leads run through my copy of Sophocles –
Oedipus : this is a sign, the pact seals my fate.
After the hospital we brought him back for the first time
– shook up in the harsh responsible ache of love –
we chose him a book to show what he meant to us :
it was too dark to see we were reading *Kidnapped* by RLS,
the lamp burned too bright to read. His escape came when
we went to the sea to see what was hilarious, each wave
crashed its comedy plates between my toes as he was thrown
across my shoulders. At last he knew that two thirds of the world
was what he thought, each time he wet himself

FREE GIFT

Before bed she said : Have you seen the slug?
I answered : I've already flossed. If I had not
misheard I would have offered to remove it.
We thought a baby was either hungry or happy
but inbetween he made a noise called SCHMIG
like a jester preparing a gig for the King of Tourettes.
We had to teach him that moral dilemmas
dreg the spontaneous & here was a case exercise :
I'd lost a nail in the cornflakes trying to scoop the free gift –
I've found the plastic prize, but should we tell anyone?

WHITE PORRIDGE, BLACK TASSLES

The white porridge swatted the floor like an albino fly.
The boy thought tugging the black tassles made this
happen – he laid the green caterpillar on its side to
make himself look taller. We'd gone crazy the night
before with a packet of bacon & a bottle of Antiguan
Rum – blind pirates of the moorless hours. But we only
gave. The summer storm tugged the GREEK GODS
wallchart from its pins – Aphrodite in the corner started
to fox – the boy thought thunder was nothing to do with
Zeus, but the snack of the world announcing its crumbs

HAUNTED LOAF

She woke me from a pollen sleep to tell me it would be a day of peace.
These hardships, spoke the sun, give us another chance :
the first bionic sea creature only made the news
because it got caught in a crab trap.
All that matrix blah of advice – but sometimes
uncles become uncles younger than their nephews.
The Question disarmed us : what were windmills for?
We worked backwards through every loaf we'd ever known
– best of boths, crustless, square – to find the answer.
Outside the democracy of the bathroom was a chart called
GREEK GODS. Things grow, she said, just watch the sun –

so with love we clipped the baby's nails to crescents
to help the gnats believe they could reach the moon

I thought the baby was George Orwell & that's why
I treated him so well. There was always a sense
of the sado-masochist about this as I once saw
a sign ALL JAZZ NOW £2 & went to the desk
to insist I paid more. I thought I still had ten minutes
left for the ONE HOUR GALLERY but the artists
were in the back drinking bottles at Polish strength.
This pushed me mainstream as I started to see the
question mark shaped tumbleweeds. Whenever I
allow someone to be served before me two things
can happen : a) the wine bottle runs dry & I wait
for the decorking of another or b) the barman forgets
my philanthopy and serves all newcomers. By the
time the ATM device says CONSENT it feels like
an arranged marriage. God kills kittens when you
think bad thoughts but sometimes it's hopeless :
she comes in topless from the grass with a grip on
some shears, above her the Vs of swifts that never
come-down. I said to her : the oggyoggyoggy is the
last refuse of the untalented; she replied : your sense
of humour is so dark you have your own apartheid.
The boy had just graduated from the University of
Snail (no career fast track but at least you would own
your own home) so we walked together the emblazoned
afternoon, through the shower room of tombstones

HOW TO GET A 6 MONTH OLD BABY INTO SHAPE

Start each day with the physical ABCs.
New moves, new letters : so now code burpees.
Cut a lemon in half & place corpuscles down in hot water,
watch the snouted rind bob like a drowned gnome.
Allow for the military rolls from couch to oak floor which
act to access a birthlike door : no pain (in utero), no gain (out utero).
A 3-wheel pram is best for picking off snails which
are both credit crunch & used gum in a piggy bank.
Remove the fish from the teapot before it gets light –
remember they have now grown too big for the spout.
Throw cotton wool at the softspot of his head :
a rorschach pawed from the fontanelle.
Although he cannot have the light you have to find
a way to give him the light. He must have the light.
As his trainer, red wine should not be among your
favourite toys – it drains the blood from your face
like rainwater down a pansy gutter. So put the plastic
tiger down before you scare it with your teeth.
You've got to teach him to treat your new shoes as pets –
which is easy : everyone treats new shoes as pets.
Watch him man the moon of gravity in the doorway bouncer,
The Sea of Tranquility is what he thinks he makes each time
he wets his napkin. Now you've got to get *compos mentis* for
the teaparty. No *habeas corpus* for anyone caught licking the dish

LEMON BLUE

We grabbed the handles of the shimmering zimmer of chance –
someone offered a box of matches called LEMON BLUE
from the stall that sold flint wheels attached to plastic steps
ridged to a range of coloured cylinders of gas. I cursed
my sloped brother of history – why hadn't he copyrighted
fire? Then came a text to say he was with whiskey & dancing
to light. I placed the phone face down on the Las Vegas
beermat, on the albino feline that never made Top Cat.
So I said to the one with only numbers behind their thoughts :
Give me something cloned to sell, to profit the sons of my only son

THE LEXICON OF PLC

He puts his head in a drum & his heart beats.
Pulls the chord on the '61 Fisher Price phone –
eyes toggle future detachments of text. Applauds
his own consultant, shares a round of teated
barley. Kisses the nurse's cheek before her operation.
Creates his own currency in the Recovery Room
of koala bear sticky labels. Stamps ants. Eats envelopes.
Teases the weasel from its box with an offer of red.
Ridicules the scale of VHS – nothing smaller? –
inverts the M of Fritz Lang to make things white,
wears a candled stetson with his druid suit to light
his dreams, hooks a snake over a GREEK GOD chart,
thinks milk is something he makes appear just
to download its disappearance. Tickles his oral syringe
with tinsel. Imagines vowels. Imagines vowels can
come in any shape, depending how much noise he makes

When the boy was incarcerated he became
convinced that a laptop broker would steal
his last labelled biscuit from the communal
kitchen. He thought the much discussed
panopticon was a poor wafer replacement.
He stared out the red LCD lights on the machine –
hand-processed shots of dolphins' eyes. Incey-
wincey shadows like 70s moths. Garish brocades
of paisley. Doctors in bowties appeared – neck
presents for patient vampyres. All lights were
men with no eyes. Jenga bricks like freights
from A-road towns, decrowned. The boy wants
to bring the Night Ward back to life as if all
previous patients failed, by choosing to leave
behind a small piece of their own silence

THE RESTRUCTURE adumbrates the playground
shepherds a schoolbell

– reaper as stand-in R.E. teacher –
shreds its own protein

of free range chicken thigh
with cellulite

What was that you –
sorry – I thought –

THE RESTRUCTURE louchely pontificates
at the Private View

peels back gouache to reveal
a dartboard sans numbers

and would be there at the opening
of a colostomy bag

to be the first to toast wet solids,
haunts the jukebox

for random credits
then edits out Last Orders.

I was watching your face
as you slept, to boxtick resemblances

sorry if you think that was rude or something
I thought it was best for you to know

THE RESTRUCTURE aims to occupy
the dictionary space for *macabre*

by attending the baby's birthday party
with a to-scale steel skull

then shadowbox like a trainee deacon,
to riffle the ABC First Reader

wearing five rings tagged
to dactyls, to begin to code

its own tactile morse for the bereft.
THE RESTRUCTURE communicates

when the connection's out –
Things were going well, I knew this would happen –

like an erotic final offer package
unread in your defunct inbox

Wake big & down dares
we all go, each step
bumps new at breath –

a big 2 now, with
a massive half, you
want to turn thumbs-down

up & make *very proud.*
These mornings in stress
wake us with songs –

beans earned in London
is where Dadda goes

Shark Attack

A shark ripped inside the bladderwrack
– a six inch scar on a twelve inch waist –
the cut organ spasms electric nets
but still he swims, saying – *kiss it better* –
and – *gone now* – anaesthetic in the icecone.
On the pre-op ward to a girl twice his age
he said – *be very brave, thumbs up* – then they
slipped on an alpha-gown to jester his fluids.
After he was born we were just glad he wasn't
green but the cyst they saw in utero was a kidney
with no route out. On the ward a surgeon
returned with another family, a post-op teenager
– beach-washed lump on a trolley-bed –
and told the family : *If you can imagine*
Medusa's head, that's what his left kidney's like :
a clump of ureters on either end of a cyst
turning incrementally to stone each year.
Surgery is the stone turner : our boy pissed
from his stomach for a year before the caterpillar
curl of his right kidney unfurled. An epidural
of morphine is no question for new parents
of a boy of two. On the night ward in the Vic-
torian hospital, no moon over the cooling towers,
no stars in the cranes, he spasms in my arms
– *make it better Dadda* – as the nurse explains
the pain is like the first contractions of labour,
Diazepam & morphine take him back to the sleep
he shocks out of, a consciousness he looks
at me from – the azure of his eyes untouched by
bloodshot – and we start the same story again
in the pauses between : *Pooh! Is that you Bertie?*

[57]

The sun threatens in whispers the gargoyles.
After we left him in theatre for the sixth time
– puppet-delicate in a taxidermist's debauch –
the anaesthetist who'd just gassed him to sleep
walked past us texting : *He's fine up there, I'm
just grabbing a coffee.* We spent the next two
hours trying on clothes for the new life we would
need. Above us on the ward ceiling a butane-filled
balloon in silverpink flounders like a dis-
embowelled John Dory. *Read dories Dadda* :
between the spasm's reflex, the nurse's obs,
the words take us out of ourselves. The catheter
emerges, a blue stent from his stomach like bait
– I'd thought that before, my God, we'd been baited –
hook, line & sinker. The tooth of a cannula bit into
his hand. A bin with instructions : *Dead Flowers
and Used Newspapers* : the poster that reads
the same each time : STOP CLEAN YOUR HANDS.
The Disney station that runs Transatlantic hours
as nurses float passed in togless blue eiderdowns
carrying biochemically engineered nightlights.

If he comes back for that tooth & tries to rip
through the Miami of your waterworks, lacerates
and thrashes over the ward floor in an Atlantis
of tentacle & fin – its face a scar unhealed
for millennia – we'll put down the story, sleep,
and let the carcharian fuck flounder in the waters
that buffed its nature. And when we get to the shore :
you've already seen we don't run, we love you forever.

How To Make Me Human

Turn the blue off my love
and start in standby. Turn
me on in red & submit
electrics. I've been talking
too long to the horrible
Third Person. I need your
breath of eaves to drop.
Turn the tap of green milk
and let the skin crease to
eyelids. The Christmas mice
have copyrighted red & gold.
When the midnight turns
let me chime dumbbells to
your poppies. Pre-treat my
meds with saffron & douse
my sheets with opium. When
I was in single mode Plato's
Forms were just applications
for the stars. The shark attack
shredded my office cortex, de-
pressed my filofax. To make me
human you pushed the ginger-
bread man biscuit cutter into
the ham. To turn on press
red & hold.

Citalopram Advent

Open this advent of no year's end
20 milligram drummerboys
behind blister-packed windows.
Can I have your sugar-coated
countdown, a treat each day
to a 25th endorphin hit
and a new start in green resolutions?
When yours ran out I broke
one of mine like a lovelocket –
you picked at the earthed collar bone
of a fortnight pack, my white
bouquet of ring-a-ring-of-roses.
Pock the pack's membrane and finger
the flour – its hare's tooth waistband.
A mouth in the soap-bar. How
the compound yawps. My tongue
never touched a navel so tasteless.
Fullstop in the analogue. My white devil.
A pocketful of posies for a one man plague.
Measure out the fruit cake this year
in Serotonin & endorphins,
share the summer salads
in signed prescriptions

and be there when

we all fall down

The Therapists

Every therapist needs to be counselled.

A man becomes aware of his own mind, cauliflowers glass quadrants – sees the roots – like a wet wart.

He talks to the therapist who listens (he is paid to listen). The therapist notes that this man has reached an impasse. Unsure how to proceed the therapist speaks to his counsellor. He echoes the impasse.

The therapist's counsellor misfires a typo into the monitor : & continues : he doesn't want to think what could become.

All the combined impasses could make a fence across the globe – thousands of men's problems mysterious as the workings of global finance. Nobody knows where they go. Each impasse. The echoes.

The man doesn't care about that. He just talks & by increments he starts to feel a little better, so that one day he leaves.

The therapist is left with the impasse – it has to go somewhere. He picks up a phone.

His counsellor turns on the screen.

And makes a call.

A call.

The Bird Cure

I was poking tarmac for mauve twenties when the kingfisher
                                        cashed its azure bullion.
It had been a long night of slow .wav downloads, then you showed
                                        me a dawn of the redwings.
I couldn't find an oak to guarantee my chequebook but you had a
                                        wren as pocketchange.
Oil had slicked my best black shoes but a starling flashed green
                                        its Pacific dorsal.
My wardrobe was for so long monotone but the goldfinch always
                                        wore the same red ruff.
I thought nothing varied more than my moods but the lakeside
                                        understood so many warblers.
Palpitations artexed a brush-in-the-eye but the woodpecker's
                                        pointillism was precise.
A heart-in-the-mouth boiled a sunnyside breakfast but the robin
                                        was a cardiac in an eggcup.
The train through the country had its own dawn plumage but the
                                        owl was a disgraced Quaker.
I thought it was just me that wore a nightsky on my back but the
                                        blackbird sheened to olive green.
The agent pitched a bachelor pad of luxury but the docks exchanged
                                        the bullfinches' shrapnel.
The pain paused its industrial estate massage while the gulls carouselled
                                        so many playgrounds.
Thoughts were muscle-sprung-to-wing but the peewit whirred
                                        itself to danger – that's what you do –
                                        take the mess away out of love.
The GP issued citalopram on the nightshift but each morning's call
                                        brought the bird cure.

THE RESTRUCTURE reminds you of a man who isn't there
who due to market dynamics wants his conkers back.

Will not, under these circumstances, share its Sunday
roast with no-marks, becomes asexual at the suggestion

of a free escort but still packs black tights
– if there's a hold-up time can be utilized –

and divides all colleagues into larks & owls
to train both to be ready for the afternoon chorus

sends obituaries by text followed with five kisses
makes emotionally intense scenes from real lives

creates a H&S package for anyone who falls on their thumbs
in the wrong fashion, stays awake for many nights

– called THE RESTRUCTURE nightwatch – to ensure its throat
remains wet (the trip-switch of conscious salivation)

then drains transparently on the pillow. *Simon's decided
to take the money & cut ship, he's had enough*

*sd Yes the jobs are ringfenced but in reality
things have changed.* Then THE RESTRUCTURE

offered a string of soundbites as advice, sd
ringfence yourself (you could be next)

ringfence your desk (with boot & mouth)
ringfence your texts (in case you mis-send)

ringfence your wife (in a single bed)
ringfence your pint (avoid expense)

ringfence for lent (it won't come back).
I couldn't believe it, the whole team went

to look for Saxon London & found only modern
rubbish in trodden layers, then got back late

to cover my break saying THE RESTRUCTURE
had taken a penny whistle to the funeral

and blew like death is just a trouser-loss & after
the coffin descended went down to the wake

signing up the mourners to a course Remembering
Manners in Moments of Crisis, *offering nibbles*

of live insects to speed up the protein fix,
recommending that to help improve their lives

they should consider giving things up, such as,
THE RESTRUCTURE *sd, snuff movies for Lent*

Pavel's 1st Art Lesson

[Points at Van Gogh] What's daaaaa?

That's a Van Gogh.

A Van Gogh.

with mousetail cobbles.
flapjack bricks.
pancake tables.
anorak waitresses.
fudgecake shadows.
ecstatic suitors.
chesspiece diners.
branch-armed boys.
piefaced horses.
sausagegreen trees.
flowerbed stars.

[Points again at Van Gogh] What's daaaaa?

That's a Van Gogh.

A Van Gogh.

with mousetail cobbles.
flapjack bricks.
pancake tables.
anorak waitresses.
fudgecake shadows.
ecstatic suitors.

chesspiece diners.
branch-armed boys.
piefaced horses.
sausagegreen trees.
flowerbed stars.

[Points left of Van Gogh] What's daaaaa?

Wallpaper.

Blue Sun

– when the sun comes up make a kiss –

– the slugs are back –

– I'm a little bit sad but happy though –

– there's a bravest boy in the world –

– open it a bit louder –

– I kiss your shave –

– the dark will go away soon –

– snowing now, must be Christmas –

– carry me through London –

– the future's got milk in it –

– look at that weather –

– good tidings for you, to you and your king –

– going to storm again –

– how about tablewhoosh –

– be very brave, thumbs up –

– there's money in the bed –

– how about juicekittens –

– need a bucket a spade & an umbrella –

– it'll be on when it starts –

– more juice on the microphone –

– I love you in this Christmas house –

– bye bye bed, good to see you –

– shadowroof –

– the blue's up now, the sun –

– Mandy Mandy in the air –

– this is a little game –

– the blue sun's come out –

– sandsmoke –

– fingers crossed the rain goes –

– I hate your lovely phone –

– colour in the black sun –

– a shellegg –

– it's very night time –

– when the rainbow comes make sand castles –

– but I want to be good now –

– the bank's not Dadda's friend –

– I'm so surprised of you –

– here's a taxi for Baby Jesus –

– the Doctor's Dadda's friend though –

– when I was a James I built a snowman like the story –

– my mouth's getting a bit happy now –

You're Meat Book

You're meat, book –
letterpress beef,
fillet of serifs,
linocut sausage
of prime conceits.

You're meat, book -
shadowwing of protein,
broadside plucked
of glyphs, shoulder
of raw mezzotints.

You're meat, book –
dictionary of diced
cuts, miscellany
of snouts & claws.
Folio lardons.

You're meat, book –
giblet cuneiform,
hog's pud of arial
and linotype. Pop-up
of cold slice & offal.

You're meat, book –
thin sliced page-
mark. Lolling errata-
slip barcoded
with inkfat.

You're meat, book –
beefheart pocket
guide. Appendix
of jerky. Crackling
slipcase.

You're meat, book.
Placenta of semiotics,
umbical acknowledge-
ments & gonad cyclo-
pedia.

You're meat, book –
veal verso &
rectal recto,
caul copertina of
gizzard's syntax.

You're meat, book –
words measured
in ounces. Off-the-
bone polemic. Epic
canapé.

You're meat book.

Book, you're steak.

THE RESTRUCTURE recommends abstention
from heroin because it gives *terrible wind*

looks down on the burst veins crawling
each colleague's nostrils thinking *busted flush*

makes mental notes to xerox their work after hours
defines plagiarism as *unacknowledged borrowing* –

and for birthday gifts invents
the Betamax Codpiece to make orgasms obsolete.

THE RESTRUCTURE creates labels for pillows
Sleeplessness May Cause Fire

responds to snail-mail with the invention
of the Out-of-Office Letter (sent 1st class).

THE RESTRUCTURE stuffs the ottoman with paralytic puppets,
defines *impossible* as "a blunderbuss that annotates"

as "a rainbow with no exchange rate" (*I know
the Cold War's over but tell Igor I love him*).

THE RESTRUCTURE doodles even in short meetings
repeats in the margins *I Monster* then snowpakes

the pain away to blister the text with white artex,
to astound with extempore generosity, lays out

a finger buffet in A&E as the patients queue
behind vending machines, cross-stitches the fabric

of kitsch & Catholicism with a free handout called
Angel Kittens (To Pray is to Purr). THE RESTRUCTURE

accepts only unique excuses for lateness such as "I was
headlocked by a ghost" & alarms its morning call

for a dawn chorus of praying kippers to sense the scale
of the possible before it wakes, then sees a darkness

in Spring, demanding payment of fish 'n' chips
by chequebook – issues glue for the walls

so the mice stick live through the night –
waving in the dawn with their arthritic high fives

Birthweights

for Freya Potts, born 22 Jan 09

When the baby arrives we announce the birthweight. To make it real. You were driving at midnight, woke us to tete-a-tete the network with Fuckin' hell : all perfect, not a freckle. So welcome Freya, at eight pounds ten.

Birth is the only operation that runs itself, medical science just helps it along. The op involves removing live flesh from flesh, undertaken not to simplify but make life more complicated. Or *various*. We take it out and watch it mould us.

One father looked back : the first time was like a bloodbath. But the last was like a bar of soap.

So welcome Freya without freckles. Is it Freya with Phoebe's face? Or the face of Potts? Or Freya with her own face, an afterthought of resemblances? All the birthweight declares is : I am here. I thought : could genetics make for babies announcing their own names in the minutes after they're born? Then the wait for the phonecall.

Past midnight, we wake. The baby's here : all perfect, not a freckle.

She says her name is Freya.

Kingfisher

It is true, it does nest with the opening year, but not on the waters

CHARLES OLSON

How do you describe the blue you've never seen?

I was fixing the biting muzzles of mitts to the Boy's fingers

you saw

– the tail-less hologram shoot its bib of ore –

I was holding the Boy from the lagoon green underbreeze of the lake

– the blue flex shook green its Atlantic dorsal –

I was persuading the Boy that faces in puddles were not the only ones to
understand him

– the savage buddha ballbearing for digested fishbone –

I was hauling the Boy's knees from the altar of logpools

– the blast of Bunsen make shrift its short fuel –

I was kneading the yeast kisses he tossed to Canada geese

– an azure lizard shed January's skin –

I was searching a path for the Boy's alchemy of chance in gold grass

– the pixelated dash from Victorian taxidermists –

I was pushing the Boy in euphorics towards the A-roads of futurist
fire services

       – the damsel blue hunter thrust its mollusc lance –

(I read, that night, *only the righteous see the kingfisher*)

    hours later, the Boy asleep,
    his consciousness given back to dreams
       – a gale to the windchimes –
    his exhausted limbs lit by the tripswitch of pulse –

    the righteous one said, as I drifted to dark
          – said the one word – *kingfisher* –
    and I caught his blue – pulled back from the only place I'd ever
                                    seen him

Nettles

Stinging hairs, there, as not there
the light around your mouth in bars –
late ambers play tricks.
Do you know the trouble this could cause?

It fucking hurts for hours afterwards
like mentally, what I do to myself –
are dock leaves apocryphal
or are we talking prescriptions?

The hairs around your mouth & jawline
softer than threads & without essences
or legacies
the danger is in what they could make me do.

The stamen of a tongue
the remembered spoken
lumps under skin for decades.

How do you explain to a boy of three
who's never been stung
that just to touch green so soft
will rash away his happiness?

Without permission he disbands school shorts
passes water in the triffid shoots
until the cod bone bristles disappear –

to explain how something that isn't there
can sting
is like his first symposium on the metaphysical heart.

Hairs so feint on a desirous tongue
that went ways outside of easiness
to first furrow for taste – then there
was someone else stood small
in the green-scented room. Someone
who blots up the time it would take us
to kiss. He sings! The words he speaks
in our breath balms the absence

as dock leaves do stings

THE RESTRUCTURE wage-labours
children to replace dictionary entries

milkfeeds gerund verbs
in the pauses between thoughts

wills its own assets toxic
to show it can go back again

elongates its huge blackness
like a furrowed owl

sends emails with subjects cyptic enough
to be re-read, such as : *2 paths* –

Come on you know I didn't mean it
like that, I only meant –

hold your love
for THE RESTRUCTURE'S take-off

hold your love like the 7 days
have lost their names

I've heard THE RESTRUCTURE wants
short-term reverse contracts

at Thanatos Plc, to spread lambrini-rumours
across the Eros Picket Fence

to say Go like the Green Man
is someone you really should meet

then to smirk its invoices, cheersing
a carafe of black tarmac.

To ask : Will you peg this virus
(to a hard copy backup)?

To ask : Will you stalk this link
(in an office with no monitors)?

To ask : Are you in to help build
horror movie carparks?

Hold your mug – I mean your love –
THE RESTRUCTURE has asked me to fuck you up

In The 'Z' Section

What we don't do will be a big mistake.
Now there's purple feathers up the staircase –
mauve fishbones from the spine of the boa
you were wearing the night you walked in me.
A false universe of stars & garters –
the constellations in my Kronenbourg
fizzing amber to multiply six months
when we would migrate to Aqua Rosa.
Then you're leaving make-up around my books
as if to make poetics go Rubiks.
Live sharks inside the breakfast egg. Red juice.
Black ice cream. O Ratty, O, O Ratty
there's paint in my tea – bother Spring cleaning.
When I was at school seagulls existed
just to shit on blazers, their narcotic
shrieks came later. It was a big mistake :
this is something else, from years before we
knew each other. Would you judge my non-self
by all those non-poems I wrote, dramatic
data-logs on feint ruled A4? I went
ways out of myself to ensure that you
never made an appearance. By the time
poetry scored through me like BLACKPOOL in
a stick of rock it was in your colour :
red with a candy bleed of deep purple.
Someone small brings me the Yellow Pages
Saying – *Read!* Saying – *Vampire Weekend!*
Have the selves we were gone ex-directory
browsing the book that only does one-route
specifics? Then we're on my parents' lawn

and you listen as I pretend to know
Chaos Theory, Infinity Theory,
the distance it takes the stars to run our
years like calendars called up a Med-
ieval library shaft. And before we shared
solipsisms there is an appointment
on your wallchart that we never kept, did
we really need to meet in The Gardeners
Arms just to give back my annotated
Talking Heads? Well no, we chose instead to
spend the rest of our lives together. You
took the Millennium Pills & Potts said
She's not sledging is she? But how could you
when you didn't yet know what *sledging* meant?
We brought in the New Year turbot white
under an indoor umbrella before
asking the taxi driver to circle
the roundabout three times for takeaways.
What would we do with food just after the
MDMA had turned our stomach to
pebblegrind & heartbeating parasites?
We'd already decided to take Jan-
uary out, slumbered for twenty one
days only dressing ourselves for parties
in Manchester : *No parties, we've done all
that, time to focus, we're through with parties –
I mean, parties obviously* . . . Last night
you couldn't sleep because you were too scared
but now it's morning in a yard of blue
– croissants in the oven, tea melding bronze –

you've come downstairs buxom in Byron's shirt.
I read *She walks in beauty like the night*
and you thought it was a good line by Suede.
These notes have filled the Z-section of your
Address Book & you say : I was planning
to go to the Jewish Cemetery opp-
osite Lidl & make friends with a mass
of Zimmermans, Kaufmanns & Rosenbergs.
Ness, I've used up all your spaces. Today's
seagulls & sunshine, next week psychosis –
to divert I ask what bird you would be
in another life & you say *hoopoe* –
I guess I was expecting more muscle
sprung-to-wing. Your body / your politics
are impossible to separate like
painted on red jeans – you cycled topless
to St Petersburg in our front room on
an exercise bike clipped with a Lenin
magnet. Could you have been so naïve to
wear such shorts? We danced to Echobelly
and went upstairs – I must have dreamt our con-
ception since. Enough to make a boy stir.
I printed off Neruda – *I can sing*
the saddest song of all tonight – and we
tacked it to the bookshelf, but what was so
apt – to say, so *sad* – in three cold bottles
of mainstream rosé & a carafe of
gin on Shrove Tuesday? You'd just got your place
and to celebrate you took a shower
but were too pissed to get out – I would have

helped but nightsuds were hard to navigate.
I followed you through Clerkenwell & Back
Hill jealous of the time someone else would
get to interview you. Sat in the Coach
and Horses tinkering a pint like an
alchemist's water sample. It took an
other year to sledge us downriver,
Dagenham's Cold War holiday camp, the
Ian Dury route through Southend to Shoe
buryness. Without witness if one of
us forgets our nuptials on the North Sea
who's to say it took place? The woman who
walked the esplanade to ask if we'd *been*
to a wedding – who was she anyway? –
the white plastic cups that took the rosé
bobcat flotsam bearded with moss & rafts
of *Lyons Maid* sticks – the jokes faded to
braille – the house falls down in new stresses &
we rebuild with each semblance of what brought
us together to begin with. The rest,
they don't say, is mystery. And the river,
old Mole, I live on it & with it &
through it & beneath it. Make a list of
what got me through this : running beside it,
writing & reading what someone else had
said : Shakespeare, Chekhov, Beckett et al. Make
that list, add : twitching, Citalopram, the
rapy. Add : the smile Pavel gave at six
weeks old after you'd left for your first night
out since birth – singe of knowing irony –

add : as my mind folded dopey meringue
– image replacing image – I bought your
Christmas presents from the German stalls on
the Southbank & found again who you were,
Russian Dolls stacked inside foetal plywood
– a pillbox ruse of red toy enclosures –
the handmade bangle, the badge, the incense.
Add : Paul Morley looking raped by Ahab
on Newsnight Review saying *we all want*
the love & life to be renewed in us.
Add : this poem by Alice Notley – 'All my
life . . . I've been waiting / to be in / this Hell . . .
with you; all I've ever / wanted, and / still
do'. The caravan's roadside & Toad says
Poop! but we hurl abuse like Ratty does :
Scoundrels! Highwaymen! Roadhogs! Add : & love.
Our sleep patterns have been rattled by Di-
flucan but stitched & ensconced now, the Boy
has met sleep – a crossroads signpost written
POPPIES beneath every arrow. The
blue gas whispers a Silly O' Clock break
fast, the 5:47 to Euston
passes gingerbread terraces without
me – the toast browns its own gold horizons
against the yard's first dawn of bereft gulls,
as you turn in bed the commute I missed
crosses the industrial reaches of
the Mersey then on through the marshes as
you upload the memory cache of these months
to a social network of zombies &

[84]

sleepwalkers. We dragged our accents back home :
is this what we mean by THE RESTRUCTURE?
And I *don't* talk about my river, you
know I don't, I *think* about it, I think
about it all the time.

Notes

LET ME SAY : This dedicatory poem is after Robert Creeley's poem 'The Crisis'

HOUSEMATES, OR HOW IT STARTS : This is a confessional poem written through a Cubist technique.

CORNWALL IN 3 TRIMESTERS : def : a trimester is a poetic form written under the duress of pregnancy. Nora is Sarah's paternal Grandmother.

WEEK 31 SCAN : obstetrician spotted a defect in the kidneys whilst the baby was in utero. This would lead to six operations in his first three years.

BLUE SUN : This is a poem made of words spoken by the boy in his first stages of language development, from 18 months to 3 and a half.

YOU'RE MEAT BOOK : After wondering for months what, in fact, they actually taught the boy at nursery and how they controlled his feral nature, all was explained when he came back one afternoon and picked up a book and said to it, intimately, 'You're Meat Book' – feigning taking a bite from it. Stanzas 7 and 8 were spoken by poet Simon Barraclough in an extempore fashion after some level of liquidation and became part of the written piece.

IN THE Z SECTION : The poem was written in Sarah's contacts' book, in the 'Z' Section. I started making notes and the whole thing grew to take over that whole part of the book. Luckily she has made no friends since beginning with Z. The poem cites moments of *The Wind in the Willows*, as remembered in the moment of writing the poem. The poem is written in ten syllable lines which was an experiment for me as I (traditionally) work in more experimental forms. The Alice Notley poem is from her book *Grave of Light: New and Selected Poems 1970–2005* (Wesleyan University Press, 2006)